EMMANUEL JOSEPH

Feast of Seasons: Celebrating Food Through Spring, Summer, Fall, and Winter

Copyright © 2025 by Emmanuel Joseph

All rights reserved. No part of this publication may be reproduced, stored or transmitted in any form or by any means, electronic, mechanical, photocopying, recording, scanning, or otherwise without written permission from the publisher. It is illegal to copy this book, post it to a website, or distribute it by any other means without permission.

First edition

This book was professionally typeset on Reedsy.
Find out more at reedsy.com

Contents

1. Chapter 1: The Awakening of Spring — 1
2. Chapter 2: The Splendor of Summer — 3
3. Chapter 3: The Harvest of Fall — 5
4. Chapter 4: The Warmth of Winter — 7
5. Chapter 5: Spring Traditions and Celebrations — 9
6. Chapter 6: Summer Bounty and Barbecues — 11
7. Chapter 7: Autumn's Harvest Festivals — 13
8. Chapter 8: The Comfort of Winter Cooking — 15
9. Chapter 9: Spring's Fresh Flavors — 17
10. Chapter 10: The Heat of Summer — 19
11. Chapter 11: Autumn's Comfort Foods — 21
12. Chapter 12: Winter's Festive Feasts — 23

1

Chapter 1: The Awakening of Spring

Spring ushers in a sense of renewal and rebirth. It's a season of color and life, and nowhere is this more apparent than in our gardens and kitchens. As the frost of winter gives way to warmer days, tender green shoots push their way through the soil. The first harvests are often simple yet bursting with fresh flavors. Imagine a spring salad composed of baby spinach, radishes, and strawberries, drizzled with a light lemon vinaigrette—each bite a celebration of new beginnings.

The tradition of spring feasts dates back centuries, rooted in the joy of new harvests and the return of life. From the Persian Nowruz to the Japanese Hanami, these celebrations honor the earth's bounty and the promise of abundance. The symbolism in the food is powerful: eggs signify fertility, while green vegetables stand for rejuvenation. Sharing meals during these times is not just about sustenance but about embracing the season's spirit.

As the days grow longer, our palates crave lighter, brighter flavors. Fresh herbs such as basil, mint, and dill become culinary stars, infusing dishes with vibrant aromas and tastes. There's a playful experimentation in the kitchen as we blend these herbs into pestos, marinades, and soups. The market stalls brim with asparagus, peas, and the first strawberries, each ingredient a reminder of the earth's awakening.

Finally, spring is a time for outdoor gatherings. Picnics and garden parties become common, where food is enjoyed under the warm, budding canopy of trees. There's an intimacy in these gatherings, a sense of community and connection that is fostered by sharing the season's freshest offerings. Every bite taken outdoors seems to encapsulate the essence of spring: fresh, hopeful, and full of promise.

2

Chapter 2: The Splendor of Summer

Summer is a season of abundance, where nature's generosity is at its peak. The days are long and the sun shines bright, coaxing a wealth of produce from the soil. Farmers' markets overflow with tomatoes, corn, berries, and melons. The vibrant colors and rich aromas are a feast for the senses, and every meal feels like a celebration. The essence of summer is captured in simple, fresh dishes that highlight the season's bounty.

One of the great joys of summer is the simplicity of its cuisine. Grilling becomes a favorite cooking method, imparting a smoky flavor to vegetables and meats alike. Picture a barbecue with friends, the air filled with the scent of sizzling corn on the cob and marinated chicken. Salads are no longer just sides but main attractions, packed with crunchy cucumbers, juicy tomatoes, and a rainbow of bell peppers, all lightly dressed in olive oil and herbs.

Summer also brings a wealth of fruits that are best enjoyed in their purest form. Sweet, sun-ripened peaches, juicy watermelons, and plump blueberries can be eaten straight from the basket, their flavors enhanced by the warmth of the sun. These fruits find their way into desserts that are light and refreshing, such as a classic strawberry shortcake or a peach cobbler. There's a delightful indulgence in enjoying these treats on a hot summer day.

This season is synonymous with gatherings and festivities. Whether it's a beachside picnic, a backyard barbecue, or a sophisticated garden party, the food is always central. Summer cuisine is meant to be shared, creating memories and strengthening bonds. The laughter, the clinking of glasses, and the communal enjoyment of food encapsulate the spirit of summer—a season of togetherness and joy.

3

Chapter 3: The Harvest of Fall

Autumn is a time of abundance and transformation. The vibrant greens of summer give way to the warm hues of gold, orange, and crimson. The air carries a crispness that signals the approaching end of the growing season. Harvest festivals are celebrated worldwide, honoring the earth's generosity. Foods become heartier, with a focus on preserving the harvest. Think of pumpkins, squash, apples, and root vegetables that are transformed into comforting dishes.

One cannot talk about fall without mentioning the comfort foods that define the season. Hearty stews, roasted vegetables, and spiced baked goods fill our kitchens with warmth and aroma. The act of cooking itself becomes a comforting ritual, a way to embrace the coziness that autumn brings. Imagine a bowl of butternut squash soup, velvety smooth and spiced with nutmeg and cinnamon—each spoonful a warm hug on a cool day.

Fall also brings the tradition of canning and preserving. Jars of homemade jams, pickles, and sauces line pantry shelves, capturing the season's flavors to be enjoyed year-round. Apples are turned into pies and crisps, their sweetness a perfect match for the spices of fall. There's a sense of satisfaction in preserving the harvest, a way of honoring the cycles of nature and the hard work of the growing season.

Gathering around the table takes on a special significance in the fall. Family and friends come together for meals that celebrate the bounty of the season.

Thanksgiving is a prime example, a holiday centered around a feast that includes turkey, stuffing, and an array of side dishes. It's a time to give thanks and to reflect on the blessings of the year. The shared meal becomes a symbol of gratitude and community.

4

Chapter 4: The Warmth of Winter

Winter is a season of reflection and rest. The earth lies dormant, and so do our gardens. The food of winter is about warmth and sustenance, providing comfort during the cold months. Root vegetables, hearty grains, and preserved foods take center stage. It's a time for slow-cooked meals that fill the home with inviting aromas. Picture a pot of beef stew simmering on the stove, its rich flavors developing over hours.

The essence of winter cuisine is found in its ability to nourish both body and soul. Soups and stews are staples, their warmth spreading from the inside out. Imagine a bowl of chicken noodle soup, the broth rich and savory, each bite offering tender chicken and perfectly cooked vegetables. These meals are often enjoyed around a fire, the flickering flames adding to the sense of coziness.

Winter is also a time for festive feasts. Holidays such as Christmas and Hanukkah are celebrated with traditional dishes that have been passed down through generations. Roast meats, baked goods, and special confections are enjoyed with family and friends. There's a sense of nostalgia in these meals, a connection to the past and to the heritage of our ancestors. Each bite is a reminder of the love and care that goes into preparing these special dishes.

In winter, food becomes a form of celebration and a source of comfort. Whether it's a simple mug of hot cocoa or an elaborate holiday feast, these moments are savored and cherished. The act of sharing food takes on deeper meaning, providing warmth and connection during the coldest months. Winter reminds us of the importance of togetherness and the joy that can be found in simple pleasures.

5

Chapter 5: Spring Traditions and Celebrations

Spring is a season rich with traditions and celebrations centered around food. Many cultures have festivals that mark the arrival of spring and the promise of new growth. These events are often characterized by special dishes that reflect the season's bounty. One such example is the Persian celebration of Nowruz, the Persian New Year, which includes a table spread with symbolic foods such as green herbs, eggs, and fish.

Easter is another spring celebration that features an array of traditional foods. From hot cross buns to roasted lamb, these dishes are steeped in symbolism and history. Eggs, a central element of Easter, represent new life and rebirth. They are often decorated and exchanged as gifts, adding a colorful and festive touch to the celebration. The Easter feast is a time for families to come together and enjoy a meal that celebrates the season.

Springtime also brings the Japanese festival of Hanami, which involves picnicking under blooming cherry blossom trees. Families and friends gather to enjoy the beauty of the blossoms while sharing bento boxes filled with seasonal delicacies such as sushi, tempura, and sakura mochi (sweet rice cakes wrapped in cherry leaves). The tradition of Hanami is a beautiful example of how food and nature are intertwined in cultural celebrations.

The Jewish festival of Passover is another significant spring tradition. The

Seder meal, which marks the beginning of Passover, includes a variety of symbolic foods such as matzo, bitter herbs, and charoset (a sweet mixture of fruits and nuts). Each item on the Seder plate has a specific meaning, and the meal itself is a time for storytelling and reflection on the themes of liberation and renewal. The Seder is a powerful reminder of the ways in which food can carry deep cultural and historical significance.

6

Chapter 6: Summer Bounty and Barbecues

Summer fruits are at their best during this season, and they shine in both savory and sweet dishes. Peaches, berries, and watermelons are enjoyed fresh or incorporated into desserts such as pies, crisps, and sorbets. The natural sweetness of these fruits is the perfect ending to a summer meal. There's a certain magic in biting into a perfectly ripe peach, its juice running down your chin, that encapsulates the essence of summer.

Summer evenings are often spent outdoors, enjoying the cooler temperatures after a hot day. This is the time for al fresco dining, with tables set up under twinkling lights or the stars. Meals are enjoyed slowly, with plenty of time for conversation and laughter. The food is simple yet delicious, allowing the flavors of the season to shine. A fresh caprese salad with tomatoes, mozzarella, and basil, drizzled with balsamic glaze, epitomizes the spirit of summer dining.

Summer is also a time for preserving the season's bounty. Jams, pickles, and sauces are made from the abundance of fruits and vegetables, capturing their flavors to be enjoyed throughout the year. There's a satisfaction in knowing that the taste of summer can be savored even in the depths of winter. The process of preserving food is a labor of love, a way to extend the joy of the season.

In essence, summer is a celebration of life and abundance. The food we enjoy during this season is a reflection of the earth's generosity. It's a time to gather with loved ones, savoring each bite and each moment. Summer reminds us to appreciate the simple pleasures, to slow down and enjoy the richness of life.

7

Chapter 7: Autumn's Harvest Festivals

Autumn is a time of gratitude and celebration, as communities come together to honor the harvest. Harvest festivals are a cherished tradition in many cultures, marking the end of the growing season and the beginning of the colder months. These festivals are often centered around food, with tables laden with the season's bounty. From Oktoberfest in Germany to Thanksgiving in the United States, these celebrations are a testament to the importance of food in our lives.

One of the most iconic autumn celebrations is Thanksgiving, a holiday that brings families together to share a meal and give thanks for the blessings of the year. The centerpiece of the Thanksgiving feast is the roasted turkey, accompanied by an array of side dishes such as stuffing, mashed potatoes, cranberry sauce, and pumpkin pie. Each dish has its own significance, representing the harvest and the traditions of the holiday.

Oktoberfest, held in Munich, Germany, is another autumn festival that celebrates the harvest. Originally a royal wedding celebration, Oktoberfest has evolved into a world-renowned festival of beer, food, and music. Traditional Bavarian dishes such as pretzels, sausages, and roast chicken are enjoyed alongside steins of beer. The festival is a lively celebration of community and culture, with food playing a central role.

In many cultures, autumn is also a time for preserving the harvest. Canning, pickling, and fermenting are common practices, allowing the flavors of the season to be enjoyed throughout the year. Apples are turned into cider, tomatoes are made into sauces, and vegetables are pickled to be enjoyed as condiments. These preservation methods are a way to honor the abundance of the harvest and to ensure that nothing goes to waste.

Autumn's harvest festivals are a reminder of the connection between food and community. They celebrate the hard work of the growing season and the generosity of the earth. These festivals are a time to come together, to share meals, and to give thanks for the blessings of the year. They remind us of the importance of tradition and the joy that can be found in sharing food with loved ones.

8

Chapter 8: The Comfort of Winter Cooking

Winter is a season that invites us to slow down and savor the comfort of home-cooked meals. The cold weather calls for hearty dishes that warm us from the inside out. Root vegetables, grains, and preserved foods become staples, providing nourishment and comfort. There's a sense of coziness in the kitchen, as pots simmer on the stove and ovens bake aromatic treats.

One of the joys of winter cooking is the use of slow-cooking methods that allow flavors to develop over time. Stews, braises, and roasts are common winter dishes, filling the home with mouthwatering aromas. Imagine a pot of beef stew, simmering for hours until the meat is tender and the vegetables are infused with rich flavors. These dishes are not only satisfying but also comforting, providing warmth on a cold day.

Baking is another cherished winter activity, with the oven providing both warmth and delicious aromas. Homemade bread, cookies, and cakes are enjoyed fresh out of the oven, their warmth adding to the coziness of the season. Traditional holiday baking, such as gingerbread cookies and fruitcakes, brings a sense of nostalgia and celebration. The act of baking is a form of self-care, a way to create moments of joy and comfort.

Winter is also a time for festive feasts that bring family and friends together.

Christmas, Hanukkah, and other winter holidays are celebrated with special meals that have been passed down through generations. Roast meats, hearty sides, and decadent desserts are enjoyed in the company of loved ones. These meals are a time to celebrate traditions, to create memories, and to enjoy the warmth of togetherness.

In essence, winter cooking is about nourishing the body and soul. It's a time to slow down, to savor the simple pleasures of home-cooked meals, and to find comfort in the warmth of the kitchen. Winter reminds us of the importance of self-care and the joy that can be found in creating and sharing food.

9

Chapter 9: Spring's Fresh Flavors

Spring is a season of renewal, and its fresh flavors reflect this sense of new beginnings. As the earth awakens from its winter slumber, the first crops of the season appear, bringing a burst of fresh, vibrant flavors to our kitchens. Tender greens, herbs, and early vegetables are the stars of spring cuisine, offering a taste of the season's promise.

One of the joys of spring cooking is the use of fresh herbs, which add brightness and complexity to dishes. Basil, mint, and dill are just a few of the herbs that flourish in the spring, infusing dishes with their aromatic flavors. Imagine a plate of spring pasta, tossed with fresh peas, asparagus, and a handful of basil leaves, finished with a drizzle of olive oil and a sprinkle of Parmesan cheese. The result is a light, refreshing dish that celebrates the season's bounty.

Spring is also a time for salads that are as beautiful as they are delicious. Baby greens, radishes, and strawberries come together in vibrant salads that are perfect for a light lunch or a refreshing side dish. These salads are often dressed with simple vinaigrettes, allowing the fresh flavors of the ingredients to shine. There's a certain elegance in these dishes, a celebration of simplicity and freshness.

The first fruits of spring are a welcome sight, bringing a sweet taste of the season. Rhubarb, strawberries, and cherries are among the early fruits that make their way into desserts such as pies, crisps, and tarts. These desserts are often light and refreshing, a perfect way to end a spring meal. The natural sweetness of the fruits, enhanced by a touch of sugar and a squeeze of lemon, is a delightful reminder of the season's abundance.

Spring's fresh flavors are a celebration of renewal and growth. They remind us of the beauty and generosity of the earth, and the joy that can be found in simple, seasonal dishes. Spring is a time to embrace freshness, to celebrate new beginnings, and to enjoy the vibrant flavors of the season.

10

Chapter 10: The Heat of Summer

Summer is a season of heat and abundance, where the sun's energy brings forth a wealth of produce. The days are long and hot, and our meals reflect the need for light, refreshing dishes that can be enjoyed in the heat. Salads, grilled vegetables, and fresh fruits become staples, offering a taste of summer's bounty.

Grilling is a favorite summer cooking method, adding a smoky flavor to vegetables, meats, and seafood. Picture a barbecue with friends, the air filled with the scent of sizzling corn on the cob, marinated chicken, and grilled peaches. The simplicity of grilling allows the natural flavors of the ingredients to shine, creating delicious, satisfying meals. These gatherings are a time to relax, to enjoy good company, and to savor the simple pleasures of summer.

Summer fruits are at their peak during this season, offering a burst of sweetness and juiciness. Berries, peaches, and melons are enjoyed fresh or incorporated into desserts such as pies, crisps, and sorbets. A bowl of mixed berries, drizzled with a touch of honey, is a simple yet delightful treat on a hot summer day. The natural sweetness of the fruits is a reminder of the abundance of the season.

Al fresco dining is a cherished summer tradition, with meals enjoyed outdoors under the warm sun or the twinkling stars. Picnics, beachside gatherings, and backyard barbecues are opportunities to connect with nature and with loved ones. The food is simple yet delicious, allowing the flavors of the season to take center stage. A fresh caprese salad with tomatoes, mozzarella, and basil, drizzled with balsamic glaze, epitomizes the spirit of summer dining.

Summer is a celebration of life and abundance. The food we enjoy during this season is a reflection of the earth's generosity. It's a time to gather with loved ones, to savor each bite, and to appreciate the richness of life. Summer reminds us to enjoy the simple pleasures, to embrace the heat, and to celebrate the abundance of the season.

11

Chapter 11: Autumn's Comfort Foods

Autumn is a season of transformation, as the vibrant greens of summer give way to the warm hues of gold, orange, and crimson. The air turns crisp, and we find comfort in hearty, warming dishes that reflect the bounty of the harvest. Root vegetables, apples, and squash become central ingredients in our kitchens, providing nourishment and warmth.

One of the delights of autumn cooking is the use of seasonal spices such as cinnamon, nutmeg, and cloves. These aromatic spices add depth and warmth to both sweet and savory dishes. Imagine a slice of pumpkin pie, its spiced filling encased in a buttery crust, or a steaming mug of apple cider, infused with cinnamon and cloves. These flavors evoke the essence of autumn, filling our homes with inviting aromas.

Soups and stews are staples of autumn cuisine, offering comfort and sustenance on cool days. A bowl of butternut squash soup, velvety and rich, is the perfect antidote to a chilly afternoon. Root vegetables such as carrots, parsnips, and sweet potatoes are roasted to perfection, their natural sweetness enhanced by the caramelization process. These dishes are hearty yet simple, celebrating the season's produce.

Autumn is also a time for baking, with apples and pumpkins taking center stage. Apple crisps, pumpkin bread, and spiced muffins are enjoyed fresh from the oven, their warmth and aroma adding to the coziness of the season.

Baking becomes a cherished ritual, a way to create moments of comfort and joy. There's a sense of nostalgia in these autumn treats, a connection to the traditions of the season.

In essence, autumn's comfort foods are a celebration of the season's abundance. They provide warmth and nourishment, inviting us to slow down and savor the simple pleasures of life. Autumn reminds us of the beauty of transformation and the joy that can be found in the heartiest of dishes.

12

Chapter 12: Winter's Festive Feasts

Winter is a season of celebration, as we gather with loved ones to enjoy festive feasts. The cold weather calls for hearty, indulgent dishes that provide comfort and joy. Traditional holiday meals are rich with history and symbolism, bringing a sense of continuity and connection to our celebrations.

One of the highlights of winter cuisine is the holiday roast. Whether it's a succulent turkey, a tender ham, or a flavorful prime rib, the roast is often the centerpiece of the festive table. These dishes are accompanied by an array of sides such as mashed potatoes, stuffing, and roasted vegetables. Each dish has its own significance, representing the abundance and generosity of the season.

Baking is an integral part of winter celebrations, with cookies, cakes, and pastries taking on special significance. Gingerbread cookies, decorated with icing and candies, are a holiday favorite, as are rich fruitcakes and buttery shortbread. The act of baking these treats is a cherished tradition, often involving family and friends in the process. The result is a delicious array of sweets that bring joy and warmth to the holiday season.

Winter feasts are also a time for traditional beverages that warm the soul. Mulled wine, spiced with cloves and cinnamon, is a festive favorite, as is hot cocoa topped with marshmallows. These drinks add to the sense of coziness and celebration, providing warmth and comfort on cold winter nights.

Sharing these beverages with loved ones creates moments of connection and joy.

In essence, winter's festive feasts are a celebration of tradition and togetherness. They bring warmth and joy to the coldest months, reminding us of the importance of connection and celebration. Winter invites us to savor the richness of life, to enjoy the comforts of home, and to create lasting memories with those we love.